# The Garbage Eater

# THE GARBAGE EATER

## POEMS
### BRETT FOSTER

TriQuarterly Books/Northwestern University Press

Evanston, Illinois

TriQuarterly Books
Northwestern University Press
www.nupress.northwestern.edu

Printed in the United States of America

10  9  8  7  6  5  4  3  2

**Library of Congress Cataloging-in-Publication Data**

Foster, Brett, 1973–
    The garbage eater : poems / Brett Foster.
        p. cm.
    ISBN 978-0-8101-2745-6 (pbk. : alk. paper)
    I. Title.
    PS3606.O7496G37 2011
    811'.6—dc22

                                                          2010044538

♾ The paper used in this publication meets the minimum requirements of the American
National Standard for Information Sciences—Permanence of Paper for Printed Library
Materials, ANSI Z39.48-1992.

This book is dedicated to Margalo Anise Foster,
for everything and more.

# CONTENTS

# III

ACKNOWLEDGMENTS

I would like to acknowledge the support of editors and staff at the following publications, where some of these poems first appeared:

*Ascent:* "At the City Church of San Francisco"
*Black Warrior Review:* "The Foreman at Rest"
*Books & Culture:* "The Little Flowers of Dan Quisenberry"
*The Christian Century:* "Via Negativa," "Longing, Lenten"
*Hudson Review:* "No Sol in California"
*Image:* "The First Request of Lazarus," "Petition: California Avenue," "Devotion: For Our Bodies," "Intercession: For My Daughter"
*Literary Imagination:* "Papyric Fragments"
*Measure:* "Geography Lesson, 1983"
*New Madrid:* "Ten Definitions Approximating Grief," "Bridal Cave"
*PN Review* (UK): "Tea with Mr. Milton"
*Poetry East:* "Afternoon Pilgrims"
*Poetry International:* "The Snow Day"
*Radix:* "The Advent Calendar"
*Raritan:* "*Lyke as a ship, that through the Ocean wyde,*" "Meditation in an Olive Garden"
*Rock & Sling:* "Contrition: Midnight Message"
*Saint Ann's Review:* "Field Trip: Two Colonies"
*Sewanee Theological Review:* "Rondeau for Plotinus"
*Southwest Review:* "An Appeal to the Ghost of Patrick Kavanagh"
*Water-Stone Review:* "Sponge Bath as Answer to the Problem of Knowledge"
*Wunderkammer:* "Final Night, in Allston"

"*Lyke as a ship, that through the Ocean wyde*" and "Parousia" were featured in *Yale Poets,* a chapbook produced by the Beinecke Rare Book and Manuscript Library (2003).

"The First Request of Lazarus" also appears in the anthologies *American Religious Poems* (Library of America, 2006) and *Best New Poets 2007* (*Meridian*/University of Virginia Press).

"Ten Definitions Approximating Grief" and "Risk" were selected for *The Poetry Center of Chicago 14th Annual Juried Reading* chapbook (2008).

A Wallace Stegner Fellowship at Stanford University allowed me to complete some of these poems and begin others. Franke, Harvey, and Whiting fellowships at Yale University were additionally helpful. The G. W. Aldeen Memorial Fund at Wheaton College and an award from the Illinois Arts Council have recently provided support during the final writing and arrangement of this volume.

My tremendous thanks to certain instrumental or ministerial readers: Jeff Galbraith, John Hollander, Jesse Zuba, Isaac Cates, Wes Davis, Rachel Wetszteon (whose memory I honor here), Kimberly Johnson, Jill Peláez Baumgaertner, Teri Jacobs—and especially—Rick Barot, Quan Barry, and David Wright.

The Garbage Eater

# The Garbage Eater

Fear of dying, fear of death:
those phobias came easy, shaped
nightly by a little boy's breath

talking out a clockwork afterlife
with parents till I fell asleep.
Most Sunday-school kids peddled
the Gospels or got lost in the deep
troughs of Apocalypse—the dead
rising, the Antichrist, the grief
or wonder, His Passion, a hundred
visions. They loved the thrill of belief;
for me, the impossible Law: I kept
reading Leviticus and felt the toll
of Numbers' rules. Eighteen and severe,
I learned to meditate on the soul's
needs. Like a desert hermit I read
Jerome's book and those Greek scrolls

of the Church Fathers, and the fear
of dying lessened, the fear of death
diminished by the Christocentric Rapture,

promise of its timeless kingdom, reign
of faithful infinitely singing there.
But unmoored grace is dangerous.
It must be guarded every hour
against the body's ignominious abuse,
the mindless evils of a worldly brain.
When I quit school, my parents made a fuss
about my teacher-leader, who explained
the stain of sin was like a gnawing whore
only killed by full attention.

I shaved my hair off, wore a wreath
to scar my forehead bloody. Under my chin
a beard hangs in a tangled mess. I'm homeless—
eat the world's crap, sleep in tarpaulin.

The physical means nothing beneath
the small fear of dying, which fears
only unworthiness more than death.

# I

. . . such as I was then, though step by step,
unwittingly, I was coming closer to it.

—Augustine, *Confessions*

# Nights of Fireworks, Days of Drought

Moonlight made the sparks less splendid,
but I still did it—lit the wick,
held it till my courage went cold,
and whipped it forward as it burst.

Then a friend's turn. Victims took ones on cheek
or neck as they ducked for cover,
scampering by instinct on rail ties.
Cinders peppered the sandbar far below.

Smell of late summer disaster in the air:
smoke spread like those Confederate spirits,
said to have floated up from the water
when the engine derailed and fell and pulled the cars.

A faraway freight whistle signaled us.
As the train approached, we called *Truce,*
scurried from our ramparts and hid
at the embankment's crest, close as we dared,

to belt the iron armor with curses
and match its screeches with our bottle rockets.
We walked home too tired to assign close calls
or complain of burns, skinned elbows.

(What use was danger but to please us?)
Never once did we think to be thankful,
nor regret what was typical,
we immortals, sneaking back through bedroom windows.

# Field Trip: Two Colonies

> Refractions of the thousand theatres, faces—
> Mysterious kitchens . . . You shall search them all.
> —Hart Crane

I grew out of small-minded clans
of dip-tossing, deer-hunter hillbillies.
Scandalous, we infested a backwater
cavity in the South, a rat-shit
state of peach-eating race haters,
debutante belles, and chain gangs
singing their exhausted souls
back to the stockade yard.
And so I sold my birthright for a song.

Because the holidays were canceled
year to year by bar fights,
street brawls, and dirt-necked
slanders, the town VFW shipped
our high school marching band
to Rowland Macy's Thanksgiving Day
Parade, New York City, where we
skunk-walked on national television,
trivial among the cartoon zeppelins.

BELTONVILLE BAND DOES GOOD
crowed the local weekly back home,
but what stuck was day-after vertigo,
us wandering rock-dumb to see
Manhattan with its pants down,
flopping its goods at the 42nd Street
Bazaar. The Amish hawked grapefruit
spoons and banana bread beside
a pack of gurus selling Persian

incense and waterworks. They gave
us free hits from the hookah
to strike a deal, the touch
of honey-apple tobacco
prancing like harem dancers
across our lips loyal to dips of Skoal.
Slightly high, we saw the Times
Square show-pimps and parroted
the *Hash-hash* stutter of drug pushers.

Later in freshman comp I'd urge
this with blood-cold conviction:
Hart Crane was a Reasonable Man,
another country boy who deified
the island, fair streets of New York,
New York, whose choiring strings gesture
everywhere, or to the eastern
boroughs at least. The threshold's here,
broadcast even on the sidewalk:

the words PORN STAR like a pair
of scars outside Rockefeller Center,
collecting all the cast-off
imprints of Westchester commuters.
And the 104 to Harlem: Midtown,
mid-afternoon. Madison Avenue
runs under us, Mad Ave signboards
run through us—Business School.
Call Now. Rembrandt at the Met.

Tapestries of the age unravel
above an old man—he's lived whole
avenues—who, seeing a hunched
and limping tortoise woman, seatless,

guides her to his. *Bless your heart,*
as she drops. *No ma'am, bless your*
*heart, bless both our hearts,* he says,
standing to lighten their shadows,
life-heavy, in the city of giants.

# Sponge Bath as Answer to the Problem of Knowledge

Learn from these art students, armed with buckets
of soap water, sponges, a fine wire brush.

They climb the ladder to the pedestal,
touch his ponderous limbs, the first lesson.

I cannot live off the life of the mind.
Should I take hikes instead, cook special meals?

History sure, sure poetry, those thoughts
of God. But everyone exists in the world;

I must acknowledge this. Even Rodin's man,
*Le Penseur,* hunched in front of the research

library with his wide, inhuman knuckles
lodged on his mouth, bows to the physical.

Brain bewildered with equations, a child
prodigy remembers that tireless night,

trying column by column to disprove
how pi unwinds into the infinite,

one lead slope of long division binding
sheets and sheets of loose-leaf. The fact itself

mattered only when she came from her room,
blood-rushed, humbled by the abstract signature.

Kneeling, they begin their seizured scrubbing
and pull the world's dirt from his bronze shins.

# The Little Flowers of Dan Quisenberry

i.m. (1953–1998)

*I've had so many good things*
*happen to me.*
      *So why not me?*

And why not there, in that relic-worthy skull, where his goodwilled
thrust and parry with the local press existed in its jocular fullness?

     *I think Christ*
*would do it that way. Or*
*Steve Garvey.*

Hardly a laureled Hall of Famer, but saintly in the modern sense, still hero
enough, emblazoned on my place mat, his submarine curveball thrown.

*No man is worth more*
    *than another, and none is worth*
       *more than $12.95.*

He'd be clutch in the ninth, seal the game after afternoon bullpen slumber:
those summer doubleheaders in the grim bubble of the Metrodome:

    *I don't think there are any good uses*
*for nuclear weapons, but this*
       *might be one.*

I-70 World Series that year, whole state euphoric, that autumn of '85.
Was a Royals victory "God's will?" Of course! Their winning meant I'd be
    assertive.

*God is concerned with hungry*
*people and justice,*
*not my saves.*

New boy in Cardinal Country, I crowed and wagged my mouth and galloped
to class wearing a plastic batter's helmet. When last bell rang I got my ass whipped.

*I'm here! It's Merry Christmas!*
*There are toys*
*in my locker. Gloves and bats and balls.*

Friend of Dad's swore Quiz was a neighbor, single men in suburban apartments.
He gave me a signed ball (real? maybe? doubtful now) for a birthday present.

*I have seen*
*the future, and it's much like the present,*
*only longer.*

No idea where that ball went. For ten years I've been reprobate, estranged
by boredom from the mediocre Royals. The game never changes, but people
change.

# The Foreman at Rest

I awoke to quick movements
in the kitchen, his late-night ritual
shortly after second shift—
almond slivers and a fresh pear
cut with grave precision into fours.
Plate set, again he would descend
into the family room, just in time
to see the final guest. I trailed
awkwardly with my sleepy steps
but was never surprising, though
emboldened I stood by his chair,
wishing every time to scare him,
who'd treat me like a regular
sharing a night. He stared straight ahead:
*That Johnny Carson's a good man.*
*Midwestern. Remember that.*
Last movie plug and curtain call
led to a canned "O say can you see?"
as a faded flag waved in the sun.
The screen went black beneath the hum,
the station's dead air already fled.

Once in a while I would recast
the almonds on that metal plate
as massive fingernails cut
from some fierce, dung-stained primate.
Later I could build them only
as the inverse, little jewelers' wares
fit for a bracelet or earrings.
When I sprinkle a handful over
a baked chicken dish I've prepared

from a newfangled cookbook,
they land just right and are delicate,
caught by a mysterious grace.
It's still this way, his midnight snack
brittle like ancient currency
made from bits of boar bone, blanched
museum pieces, curiosities.

Now to hear again how he tapped
a pack of Winstons on his wrist,
I accept the memoir's sentence:
there coated thick with garish strokes,
here purified to monologue.
How does one realize the portrait
when the living man was missed
the first time? Thirsting for detail,
I want to notice the juice
on that pear, half-eaten and still
glistening in the lamplight.

# Geography Lesson, 1983

Immigrant kids in a Midwest classroom,
we were the plural in the word *passersby.*
Our heartland marked the X of the nation,
from La Mesa to Maine, Seattle to St. Augustine,
and us—obedient children of interstates
cradled by a continent's cross-stitch, groomed
parochially. Each coastal city
buzzed in distant zones, like flies against a screen.

# Passage

... he dreamed that a certaine man stoode by him, and bade him,
God spede, and calling him by name, sayd to him, "Caedmon,
I pray thee singe me a songe." Whereto he made awnswere and
sayd, "I can not singe. For that is the matter why I came owt from
the table to this place here, because I cowld not singe." "But yet,"
quoth he againe that spake with him, "thou hast somewhat to
syng to me." "What shall I syng?" quoth he. "Sing," quoth the
other, "the begynning of all creatures." ...

—*The History of the Churche of Englande.* Compiled by
Venerable Bede, Englishman. Translated out of Latin into
English by Thomas Stapleton Student in Divinitie (1565)

*Word said, Promethean fire,*
*Altamira's cave walls lit*
*for an hour, the Ark, the Argo, Ur,*
*iron, papyrus, maps and arrow,*
*Code of Hammurabi, rope, ships,*
*Sumerian numerals, potter's wheel*

And in the end it's instinct,
it's in the species. These two
brothers for instance. Tonight,
Greek diner: I overhear
them two booths over. They speak
quick, in businessmen's fashion.
Maybe nature's after us,
I think, imagine their act,
their display before family.
Premature gray says, *This time,*
*This time* . . .

*China's triangle theories, Theban*
*obelisks, Etruscan chariots, fabric*
*dyes from purple snails, acacia wood,*
*olive oil, ram skins, lampstands,*
*Solomon's cedared Temple, Hanging*
*Gardens, the Sphinx, cranks, aqueducts*

They're entrepreneurs,
embryonic, and intend to open
a baseball store. Just a shop
full of vats of baseballs, no
bats, cleats, or jackets. It'll change
the face of each mall, one says.
But they're still stuck on the name
for dream: *Big Balls* is "too much."
*Lotsa Balls,* one guy foresees,
numen swept up in vision,
"has the right spin." *Balls du Jour*
is the pleased counter, offered
with serifs for the culture,
sad hint suggesting the men
they meant to become, the ones
they have not.

*water clocks, mercy seats, clay tablets*
*of Mesopotamia, lock and key, Jericho,*
*carpenter's square, the pontoon*
*bridge of Darius, gears, cataracts,*
*basin irrigation, the Archimedean*
*screw, geometric roots, roads, soap*

But I've heard other stories
of bright wonder transumed from modesty—
fitful progress, gradual rise,
obsessed humanist, the bard
who wins the last line and dies.

These pins and monuments go back so far:
paddleboats, Alexander's
Library, whose scrolls declared
"the five machines of the age"—

*lever, wedge, pulley, screw,*
*and cogwheel,*

Armada, medina, cathedral:
We build the kingdoms. The proof?

One friend, fronting an acid-jazz ensemble,
says, "We riff, I sing these tunes,
songs about love and destruction and stuff."
Isn't that measurable?
Chamber piece in Brueghel's tower?
Some belabored thing risen
obliquely from black waters,
bearing burdens sweetly felt?
Then a deeper meaning comes,
the heaviest, settling here
to forgive all urgency,
spare the harvest, bless this pair
in pilgrimage—woman mild
at heart who falls ill, or discredited
man, helpless, weeping in side
streets of a spendthrift city.

*test test test the spirits test*
*the spirits test*

                    So how was I to know
these brothers were explorers
(were us once, in other words)
born against another life
to learn insistence must ebb,

as the tideline lapping sand
beyond the levees where we used to toil?
Old enough to seize real tools,
too young to recognize the bitter seed
of an uncle's mockery
grating the screen of the porch,
that flood summer they described
a marvel, *Bridge of Ages,*
then began the channeling
after Sunday's homily,
grown dumbly timid, faded
into June humidity.
By twilight they had emptied
six feet of mineral-rich river soil
from the portal. White shirts stained,
these boys sweated out ambition,
with desperate equations
strayed beyond the physical
(world we're always told about,
deprived of proclivities).
We find the kingdoms.

                They struck
the mouth like human pistons,
powerful ones with minds afire,
then stopped and stuck their shovels
in the mound beside the pit,
their corridor to Asia.
The grown-ups' horseplay never slowed them down,
as the failing light hovered
like parsimonious thought
over the deposit and enclosure.
And in the frenzied spirit
of Aswan and Panama,

they soon dreamt of Chinamen and a sun
rising in Taiwan, then turned
again to earth to dig their youth away,
closing the line between them.

## Lyke as a ship, that through the Ocean wyde

I take a taxi to the DMV
on free weekdays, and like a stowaway
observe the goings-on, this long ennui.
Too many lines inch forward to convey
futility at 10 A.M.—"Come stay
awhile and meet some interesting folks,"
joked one employee on the phone that day.
They stare, endure the PA drone, and coax
returning predecessors like an axle's spokes.

Across the room someone hollers at a clerk:
a drunken driver unforgiven here,
debilitated by the paperwork.
I've come to learn the desperate straits they steer,
the necessary clarities that jeer
at them through clipboards, forms, the March head cold.
They swear and groan, then sigh and disappear.
Another guy who's recently paroled
desires renewal. He does everything he's told.

Young people with their nervous thumbs await
the fifteen minutes that will change their lives.
Stiff permits serve as amulets of state.
The overweight instructor soon arrives
to terrify the sophomore when he drives.
Successful ones display their toothy grins
and from the photo booth pass friends high fives.
Two ovals stain that navy screen. The lens
can't see the dirty torso where the soul begins.

# Via Negativa

It took time to make these several lines
and leave them free of all that might have been.
What sacrifice this requires, what delight,
ascetic yet privileged, to leave it upright
like a Chinese box or a house of cards.
This could have been many things: the barren
field of elegy, a mass sung at Lourdes,
or some harmonious bed made of chords.
Instead, it celebrates its reticence.

He took extraordinary and peculiar pleasure in looking at things in
which there was any mark of beauty or adornment. He never ceased to
wonder at old men who were endowed with dignity of countenance,
and unimpaired and vigorous, and he proclaimed that he honoured
them as "delights of nature." He declared that quadrupeds, birds, and
other living things of outstanding beauty were worthy of benevolence
because by the very distinction of their nature they deserved favour.

—*Leonis Baptistae de Albertis vita*

# An Appeal to the Ghost of Patrick Kavanagh

These lines, plain as the silent fields
you ploughed as the hours fell to sunset,
have neither the nerve of those severe
four-faced angels shown to Ezekiel,
nor the pure, symmetrical minuet
that scales the marveled arc of violins
in Handel's *Largo.* Even the gray-haired
folk-house guitar player who fights
to lay all the notes out right surely
performs a more auspicious act tonight,
eyes closed tightly, tracing perfectly
this basement stage behind the square
that hosts his quiet coronation.

But if they may, let the words glide
through the air like a mower's blade,
working at harvest to reap the crops,
or let them turn and take the shape
of a young and clumsy farmer's blunt
corkscrew tools, little spades that glint
as they prod the dark earth of the heart,
or gloved hands that—moving the soil
still covering the yield—scrape apart
the clods above the star-nosed mole.

# Ten Definitions Approximating Grief

—for Frank Hogrebe

It's about to be born of the voice, the hysterical caller recorded
    on the emergency line.
For this reason convenience stores are dangerous, often robbed
    despite the hint of moonlight.
And the man slowly smoking that cigarette at the darkened rest stop
    off the interstate—he himself
maintains its stoic version: sparks expire across the parking lot
    as the heavy hours pass.
It haunts the moments before work, the days victimized by violent
    weather, the one-room nights.
Through the thin wall Pico della Mirandola tries to deny its existence,
    says Man, being the center of hierarchy,
is the molder of his own destiny. It suppresses the sound rain makes.
    It applauds the minor notes,
finds residence in the keys of the composer's final piano concerto.
    The theologian who accused
Tertullian of possessing "extreme and rigorous views" has never known it.
    The three-legged dog defeats its
greatest manifestation, and though absent in Hegel's *Phenomenology of Spirit,*
    the director of Special Persons' Camp
sees it always, to see it fall away—farmhouse, roadside morning
    glory—and says there and there and there.

# Final Night, in Allston

And trees unrooted left their place
—John Dryden


Let this line be the arrow
              returning us both
       to that time on Commonwealth
when we drank placebos,

dreamt of Vermont farms
              and talked about operas
       I knew nothing of. You gave arias
special resonance and form,

explained with great passion
              theories of the spheres.
       Consider this: I even seemed to hear
celestial humming risen

above the buzz of other barflies
              and the cherrywood facade.
       We needed one more cider for the road
to hide from what we realized.

# Trashy Elegy for the Queen of Shock Rock

There was nothing
she wouldn't do
fifteen years ago:
Irrepressibly the ego
begets flamboyant business.
Duct-taped nipples

or clothespins pinching.
Teased mohawk means
she does drugs.
*Put your love in me*
she sneers, chain-saw
teeth gnarling guitars.

The music sucks,
but disappoints? Never.
Plasmatics album covers
make young loins
quiver with sensation,
help us imagine

what wild spirit
flaunts that body.
Oh yeah, right.
Could fantasy happen,
she'd surely terrify
us to tears.

When the band
vanished, she made
lesbian jail movies.
Sexpot, icon, animal
activist. Last words—
*no self, only calm*

# Evening When the Secret Vanished

Afterwards he told her what the doctor said
and surmised, and promised
like mother with child to keep his strength,
to suffer the long-winded pageant
of specialists waving their diagnostic banners.

She recognized the night's unusual details,
failed the fathoming. Why
this place, the hour's drive, his grave politeness?
She noticed lipstick traces on her water glass,
asparagus head buried in a bed of lettuce.

In a cove at sunset in a crescent bay
the secret vanished, and if
not wholly gone then opened within itself
more fully, with dreadful folding, a pair
of enclosures over the one stark truth.

He gave her the news he'd harbored to live
with these few weeks. His speech
suspicious of confusion, he confessed
none of the stunned or aghast business
of possible losing. Words not lost but hidden

gain the more aware regions: this sad man
locked in a body's solitude,
and around him, huddled forms of foothills,
the surf's white agate points, and moonlight
like an unction covering the face of water.

# Risk

Adrift she awoke one morning, and then
crash-landed in a different life—mangled, baffled,
left helpless in Reason by sharp whippings of pain.
The muscles torqued her arms like corkscrews,
                    one inward, one outward.
Her father found her whimpering, fallen from the bed.
Eleven years old that week.
    Focal lesions, torsion spasms: too much charge
in one of the brain's quadrants, so the tendons never loosen,
no slack in the sinews.
Soon the tautness moves beneath the chest. The neck, the jaws
cannot withstand the lunge and twist of ligaments contorting.
The head takes its freakish angles
                     and she ceases to speak.

    And so on for ten years,
disease not diagnosed. But there is progress. Still,
immeasurable cost of what falls away: no more school days
as she knew them, no cars or dances, any plan (whether for tomorrow
or college or the ages after) affected forever.
Some friends turn away, presumably.
Double mortgage, a lost job of her mother's. Were she older,
there would be a lover, one hopes, to comfort his bewildered
                 love, but possibly not.
Kinetic dystonia, *musculorum deformans,* tension in the basal ganglia.
      Near Turin, a teenage girl studies to become
a neurosurgeon. Her mother thinks it improper, her daughter like a man.
Every expectation *not* met, all that is overlooked for its sake,
this disapproved-of calling.

First the hiss to leak the local anesthesia. The surgeon,
overworked mother far from the Dora Riparia, drills into
her patient's skull, widens the hole with a corkscrew,
and sounds the inside,
at microscopic intervals, for a clump of cells swollen
                              by electric overcharge.
She locates the spot and puts a regulating electrode
at its core. At the far end of the table, a red bulb glows mildly,
attached to the right big toe. Its constant light communicates
a kind of patience to assistants tracing vital signs.
            She is conscious throughout the procedure, decidedly awake
when a nurse asks how she feels. It seems dream-willed. One day later
she is better, smiling from her second face.

            Tired of course, sore and groggy from surgery, dumpy
from the analgesic numbness, an impression of stress fracture
from traveling boldly through nonsense toward the cortex,
scalp peeled back, brain's lamina gleaming, cerebellum beating
like a larger sister to the heart,
                        unperturbed by its exposure,
gobbling oxygen. They activate the gadget, and a silver spark flickers
in her left eye. For the first time with a woman's arms,
she leisurely holds them out straight, palms up in blossom.
            Because she's suffered, because there exists
*technique* that can approximate miracle, normal feeling feels
unearthly in its ease. Above the recovery-room haze, the family
china taken again to the table: settings silent, gait stable,
no tremble, not an inch.

# The First Request of Lazarus

## 1

> . . . so newly separated
> From the old fire of Heaven.
> —Ovid

Already weary
from second living, new
dying of renewed patience,

old Lazarus of Bethany
betrays the uplift, desperate
for a death pregnant

with meaning, reliable passing.
How does one return,
happily, to work the olive groves?

How to age now? Even feasts
felt nebulous, and villages—
he seemed beyond them. True,

nothing terrifies like that
desertion: fading one
swallowed in the cave mouth,

linen strips to bind
the limbs. Though loss like this,
however uniquely it strikes

the forsaken, is ordinary still,
more familiar than altars,
fruitful as peasant markets.

# 2

. . . there is nothing
But howling wind and solitary birds.
—William Butler Yeats


This Lazarus, body rich
with sickness, deathbed-ridden,
spoke of spent candles,

tabernacles, frankincense.
Dogs licked his sores.
His suffering justified

the rage, his matted beard,
the pure fear. Ah, the tomb's
thick silence: its air balmed

his aches like lanolin. Those days
undenied, then the honor—
a *rabbi's* tears as he bid

the boulder gone. He staggered
toward the stone aperture,
face wrapped in canvas.

Sisters could not barter grief
so quickly. Younger ones were called,
their return more painful.

They also know desire:
daughter of the synagogue ruler,
the widow's son at Nain.

# 3

Changed from glory into glory,
Till in heaven we take our place . . .
—Charles Wesley

As for him, he waits—
impatient, stone-jawed, face hanging
like spoiled fish. He gainsays

symbolism. He knows at last
we are destined for this,
we serve one purpose, fatally,

make good on this clay-made
existence only in keeping
our good, last word.

Ether, end breath. Mindless
derelictions near soliloquy, twice
uttered. Truth is less beautiful

in rehearsal. This vocation
serves an instant, laid for everyone.
Then, only then, would the earth

surrender its mortal turning,
open wide the oceans
to let its inhabitants pass,

carrying clumsy dynasties,
their destinations somewhere
otherwise, and not here.

# Afternoon Pilgrims

O may my body sink back to that life-giving soil.
—Miklós Radnóti


Four buses later, the adventure's just
half-finished: we admire the silent figure
along the roadside. Bronzed, his trench coat tossed
by imagined winds, he judges the century

into which he'd been born. Heat sidewinds
across the access road, records our search.
Respects paid, Abda has forgotten marches
for markets: leather, wicker, fruit. We tend

our hunger with a plum and peach, then scout
the Rabca's banks, two grave chasers on a quest.
"Morbid" you said. You'll howl, but I recall

most clearly that peach: juice, taste, the rest,
yes, each bite a downbeat. History-bloodied roots
resume their music. Meters ring like distant bells.

# Meditation in an Olive Garden

No Mencius-threaded grove restful with panpipes and shepherd life,
just the chain restaurant off Sherman Street. But the manager
intends to make me think so—pastas on the posters, carafes
of Mantuan wine lined up by shades of red and gold and white.
In Palo Alto, Sunday sunlight stimulates the atmosphere
as do the lively, prerecorded violins' piazza overtures.

I order a moscatelli entree a million people eat every day,
all over this country, maybe other countries. When I see them
or hear them first, desultory, skimming the window above me,
they compel my eyes to follow their itinerant alighting,
flies the size of quarters, persuasively large, let's say.
Just two to begin with. Soon four, five, then seven. Four wings

fine, unclean but bearable, but fourteen—lord, sixteen!—what grim
numbers. Their aggregate weight is greater than my silverware's.
The place continues its mendacious ways, but with a certain clarity:
Off to a Brecht play this evening; his "defamiliarizing" starts early.
After the Caesar salad, breadsticks, a second drink,
my appetite's like a wrinkled bean. I'm glued to the base theater

of the flies, how one rubs its back legs like a scout with kindling,
pinpoint of candlelight coming; one dumbly enticed by my face;
another at a more investigative pace, with every hop-step soils
the pane where it lands, or is that merely insect fiction?
My fellow gourmands willfully keep their gazes on the table.
Scrutiny reveals the bantam escort of a gnat, barely visible.

They inch onward in tandem as a tugboat leads a cruise ship,
or a satellite orbiting Jupiter, choose your disproportion.
Outside the window sits a spider—untroubled, his underside displayed
to me, this atomic flock of flies, and our embarrassed waiter,
mumbling something about more water. "Yeah, and a stun gun
or billy club please." He brings a coffee to apologize, which I sip

from twice, and a slice of cheesecake. The spider's legs look
immense and long from this angle. Their bent joints form looming buttresses
above the abdomen. Under this small, dormant cathedral
stirs the flies' mindless, honest enterprise.
I think of the untouched cake, taken to the kitchen, thrown away,
of the cabaret (not Brecht's at all) whose songs exaggerate his worker's zeal.

It's been one week and near my neck I hear their buzzing still.

# Part-Time Work at Coffee Bars

*—a frasca*


She said she'd stay. I fear I've been abandoned.
    Today I saw her with another manager.

# No Sol in California

California when it's cloudy is the saddest
place on earth, a broken promise,
something scurrilous beneath the palm trees,
or the stiff-necked eucalyptus flagging.
When it is overcast we're castaways,
gray and grim-faced and mocked by all
we surround ourselves with: the useless
pools, the sunglass huts, fruity color schemes
aflame on restaurant billboards, red convertibles
speeding on Highway 101—all ephemeral.
We depress ourselves with the smell of rain,
outdoor jobs, a squall off the bay, the tube says.

The way the skin looks takes getting used to,
tan lines less apparent, veiled by a matte
despite the sweat. I drive along a parkway,
and realize how the fate of every day
depends upon the gleam off the bumpers
ahead of me, a need for the need of sunroofs.
The letters of street names dim a little bit,
claims abandoned by the coming front:
Sunset Lane, Sunnyvale, Sunrise Estates,
Sunshine Gardens, or just plain Sun Street.
These, the first figures of despondency.
No shadows splice stucco or cool terra-cotta,
already obscured in visible gloom.
It's hard to wake in a cavernous room,
then wait, passionless, for the bus.

As in the ancient Grecian foothills,
these cities are the temples in which we
consecrate ourselves to whatever Master:
Give your faithful, bronzed creation solace.
Let not the pyx be empty, nor my day
like an insufficient altar, my house
braced against burglars, all the lights shining
and nobody home.

# Petition: California Avenue

Taped to a red
"College/Career Info"
catalog box

near this block's
crowded sidewalk bistro,
one business envelope.

*Please pray*
*for my husband Cliff*
*for his health. He is very, very ill.*

*God loves you,*
*Dedra.* Maybe hung just
that day, ten minutes since.

Looks more like a week,
open but not torn,
faded script & weather warps.

Any money inside?
A single dollar there
not taken, or

left in the first place
to fight a cryptic sickness
for a stranger's sake?

Even change would help,
I guess. I try to make myself
think so, feeling otherwise.

Yet prayer requests
don't burst or surface
unless engendering pressures rise.

What saint didn't realize this?
Overriding fissure
holds no force enough

for prayer purely, praise alone.
Petition then, as when a desperate woman
appends a space for coins

and bills to swell her plea
with evidence, merest
sustenance of passersby.

Walking on comes simply
in the face of such an offering,
such speculative currency.

I barely stopped, curious only,
if the truth be known,
and will never know

if anonymous alms
were given, or if in time
they would be.

I didn't leave a dime.
What I venture, waiting
at a four-way, may displace

full disregard, or hardly.
Test the spirits: hastily entreat
the Lord, with effortless devotion.

Her crisis meets the half heart
of soulful caring, my fleeting
street-corner prayer.

# Parousia

—Gates Computer Science Building, Stanford, California,
Anno. Dom. MCMXCVI

Temples still adorned with ravishing ornament.
      Refulgent with gifts, dedicated to
what have you.

Nods to old emblems: cornice and verdigris
house the incense of calculus
wafting through immaculate, dimly lit hallways.

A painter converts
a barn into commodious studio,
      hayloft and high-ceilinged. It is very good.

      The days will come
when not one stone will be left upon another.
Save this now,

stately Hoover Tower's first-floor display
glosses Great Depression thus: Blame it on
      dumb Coolidge . . . the klutz.

      Let this be inscribed
      in the scrolls of the land, as a stylus
glides across Pentium-fed Palm Pilot:

"Isn't it plain to all—
      *be thou my confusion*
      —that these mounds were palaces?"

Nation will rise against nation and kingdoms
do battle. Enormous earthquakes,
heaven's signs. There will be opportunities

to testify. Truly, truly.

# At the City Church of San Francisco

Not a thousand tongues singing this morning,
but enough to fill up the little space,
Main Post Chapel of the Presidio,

lovely, if only temporary home
for the gathered, this young body of Christ,
new church which soon will need someplace bigger.

Attending with friends, themselves becoming
members this service, I want to follow
like one who has relinquished everything,

but struggle just to get the hymns right, or
understand the passage from Luke's Gospel.
How to preach with so much that's beautiful

around us? Sunlight heating the sandstone,
red brick of the military buildings
stately and from another century,

Golden Gate in the distance, those orange altars,
the bay beyond with its long, silver wings,
and perfect bursts of plant life everywhere—

I saw these things just walking from the car.
The pastor is a man of faith indeed,
attempting exegesis in the midst of this.

I try to resist as they go forward,
focus on the chancel rail they walk toward.
But as they raise their hands to take the pledge,

my eyes seize the motion just below
the sanctuary beams. Shadows of eucalyptus
or transplanted cypress pass over

a lone panel of stained glass like river
water across smooth, prismatic rock,
dimpling with light an androgynous saint,

animate, zealous for the cause, hungry
to cheer the tired ones, heal the invalids,
and the standing lead hobbling to the kingdom.

. . . For no man's life standeth in the abundance of the things which he possesseth. And he put forth a similitude unto them saying: . . .

—The Gospel of St. Luke 12:15–16 (Tyndale's version)

# Devotion: For Our Bodies

Yes love, I must confess I'm at it again,
struggling in vain with my Greek declensions.
I know it's common, but I want to show
you what I found in *Praxeis Apostolon,*

chapter one, verse twenty-four: this exquisite
epithet, *kardiognosta.* Forget
briefly its context, that the Eleven,
genuflecting, implore the Lord to give

wisdom. Between Justus and Matthias,
who replaces Judas? Let this word pass
to private sharpness toward love's dominion.
Let me kiss it across your collarbones—

*knower of hearts.* Its sweetness fills my mouth
and our twin lots, as if they'd chosen both.

# Papyric Fragments

*A letter from wife to husband. 168 B.C.*

Isias to her Hephaestion, greeting.
If you are well and all [                    ]
still well, it accords with my prayers
to the gods. Your child is healthy,
and all the household, and I myself.
I read your letter from Horus—you too,
detained in the Serapeum at Memphis.
But others have come home. Where
are you? I am thoroughly displeased,
and your poor mother is annoyed too.
[                              ] sent nothing during
such critical days? If nothing pressing
keeps you, please return to the city.
Do me just one favor by taking good
care of your bodily health. Good-bye.
Year 2, Epeiph 30.

\*\*\*\*\*

*A son's letter. Second century B.C.*

Diogenes to Hicetas. Father, do not
be upset that I am called a dog [
    ]coarse cloak, a staff in my hand.
You should rather be glad, your son
is satisfied with so little. [   ]
take heart, since the dog is protected
by the gods themselves, his clothes
the gods' invention.

*A toll receipt.* A.D. *75*

Sarapion has paid the one percent
tax for toll dues of the Oasis upon
one ass-load of barley and one ass-
load of garlic. Let him pass. The 2nd
year of Vespasianus, seventh (7th)
day of Mecheir.

*****

*A notice of death.* A.D. *151*

To Melanus, [

                ] my father Psoiphis,
son of Paopis and of Asis, of the said village,
exempted priest of the said temple, has died
in the month of Tubi of this present 14th year
of Antoninus Caesar the lord. I [         ]
notice that this name may be struck off, and I
swear by Fortune that the given record is true.
[

                              ]
this 14th year of the Emperor Caesar Titus
Aelius Hadrianus Antoninus Augustus Pius.

*****

*A question addressed to an oracle.* A.D. *25*

O lord Helios, beneficient one,
say if it is fitting that Phanias

and his wife [                    ]
not to agree now with his father,
but oppose him and will not
make a contract. Tell me this
truly. Good-bye.


*****


*A letter from husband to wife. 1 B.C.*

Hilarion to his beloved Alis very many
greetings. We are still in Alexandria
and [
                                        ]
but do not be anxious. When I receive
my pay, I will surely send it up to you.
I beg and entreat you, take special care
of the little one. If by chance you bear
a child, if it is a boy, let it be, if a girl,
cast it out. [
        ] Aphrodisias said you said,
"Do not forget me." Could I forget you?
Then I beg you, do not be anxious.

# Aubade, with Samara

Had we held all the elements
between us in our bare hands,
the way the rainwater was

captured in a plastic cup
set carelessly upon the sill—
morning of country wonder,

the thrill of discovery there—
would our blind deliberations
have finally been fulfilled?

But I've come to love you more
in bearing your not being here.
So would so many answers,

then, have made us abandon
each other even faster,
both as desperate as the two

tattered wings of that hope
sent forth leap-of-faith
from sugar maples? One seed

spared everything to float,
to meet the cup's clear aftermath
still fighting toward the sunrise.

# Bridal Cave

"Strange is your image," he said, "and your prisoners strange."

They come in heavy numbers to be wed
inside the darkest recess of the Ozarks.
Geologic altars presuppose the clerks
outside the cave mouth, bundling birdseed.
She's said no to go-karts, strip malls are passé,
so between the type of place and time of year
he becomes an artificial paramour.
(Maybe they're just impulsive, who's to say?)
Summer blooms in sunken grottos. Bouquets
and pinwheels, still as pools, reassume
their glimmer in the subterranean gloom.
Descending, lovers leave the cabaret

as organ music fills the cavern. He says
a quick "I do" to the future matriarch.
After the recessional, groomsmen shark
upon bridesmaids; one stand-in wears a fez.
A swift reception's free of monograms:
one dispenses napkins, the champagne's snatched
from Coleman coolers. Portrait artists catch
tuxedos and stalactites in their frames.
Returning to the surface, he decides
he can get used to this idea, this wife.
Rice and sunlight tint her hair with new life,
this dream Eurydice smiling at his side.

# Sestina for One Coast

—an epithalamion for I & M

*Antonio:*
No wonder San Francisco needed fire.
Cloaked in sea mist like the city, my mind
was encumbered. I struggled to commit
one lonely, noble act. But a pavilion's
cornerstone gave weight to daydreams; the bay
became a field where altars scored the waves.

*Mellinda:*
Across a continent the sound of waves
breaking, quiet as parting sighs, conjured the fire
that set the horizon blazing on the bay,
and while you wrestled angels in your mind,
I sat waiting in a grand pavilion,
Chesapeake immaculate, to commit

absolutely. Yet you could not commit
this way, with a forceful abandon that waves
away the shell, an empty pavilion
full of cobwebs, host to a dwindling fire.
Shells fortify the self but kill the mind:
Dead, but—Safe. So you kept desire at bay.

*Antonio:*
You had to suffer yours—renounce the bay's
possibility, my "thought" to commit.
I loved the lover only in the mind.
I dreamed in colors of water, but waves
themselves were foreign. You were a growing fire
inside the philosopher's dream pavilion.

That was the problem—an abstract pavilion!
Silent and numinous beside the bay,
my shelter couldn't undergo your fire.
So I tried to go without you, commit
myself to earnest things. But the cool waves
rolled against my skin and purified the mind.

*Mellinda:*
Water cleared your heart, fused spirit to mind.
You found me hesitant in my pavilion,
which stood until I said, *Yes.* Then the waves
pummeled the walls and sent the remnant to the bay.
I had decided, like you, to commit
a pure, substantial heart refined by fire.

*Antonio:*
And now our minds like ever-present fire
forge a new pavilion where we commit
ourselves, two waves whose crests outgrew the bay.

# New Territories

Because so much commotion was to come
with her remarkable life and us to witness it,
I chose to ease into another strangeness
(women's secret, doctor visits so mysterious
to men) by joining you at the ob-gyn,
where we sustained the early pregnancy.
Doing our best to share responsibility,
we made a spiral notebook heavy with questions.
But I became a squirrelly, curious child
enthralled by the names in this sort of museum.
What *is* a Climara transdermal system?
(Three appointments now and I still don't know.)
The smallest detail mesmerizes me:
solution cup in which the Pap smear's swished,
the sound reminding me of mouthwash. (*Let it go!*)
And stirrup covers, what cute little booties!
No male could ever have invented such
decent, quaint devices—screen-printed logos,
elastic sewn in the hems. How so many flats
and pumps have put a day's dirt on that white cotton.
How so rapidly we'd get used to them,
those tiny, rumpled booties.

# A Confession Kind of, a Kind of Prayer

> And prey on garbage.
> But soft, methinks I scent the morning air.
> —*Hamlet*


When he calls collect from Times Square,
I understand how he's made good
on all those brags and actions that defined
the bonding of our high school days.

I was Brag and he was Action. He'd beg
me to keep up, to bag this girl
and scam that one, steal cigarettes,
sneak out back doors with Dad's peach schnapps
wrapped in my coat. Even then I couldn't
follow such wholehearted pleasure-seeking,
much as I wished. His desire insatiable,
at times—hateful, the way he'd play
all roles till the car ride, quotidian,
where he'd take his junior-high fawns
five years his younger (I see their doll's eyes),
love them with the pure force that marks
a tyrant's love-logic. His deeds
left me speechless, and envious. I was
stuck in student council, like some clean-bean
"Sandy" from *Grease*. Dissatisfied, I cared
about my reputation like a sentence
in which good reasons lay, parenthetical.

So why be surprised, after all these years,
to hear he's living in a smoke-filled room
with a peep-show stripper? Just kicked
out tonight, stunned. It's made him sound older.

He'd never let it happen so before,
was the one to terminate the bang. *Rocked
by my dick!* he still exclaims, an attempt
to shed volition like a skin.
Because he always was All Will,
he'd kill for a new start, or for what was
or might have been. (That tense, it sounds foreign.)
*But not to worry!* laughingly.
He bays his enduring mantra:
*Don't lose the spirit! Don't go limp
on Glory!* Silly.
We reminisce, he promises
a new address, and then the line goes dead.

Sometimes I can miss it too, I admit.
Married now, a child on the way,
every day I teach kids to read
(or, let's be honest, just watch them awhile)
in remedial class. His disregard
charms still: how far his passion seems
beyond me. Does the longing ever stop,
or will the secret stair feel less severe
on the knees? Why care? I desire
a different degree of glory,
tireless and potent in its quiet life.

# Tea with Mr. Milton

I often imagine a post-Pentecost
fete where every word is sturdy and not a phrase
is lost among the guests. Even idiom earns applause,
   which sends me to the next best

   conjecture: mahogany-paneled room
full of English speakers gathered from across the years.
*Sundry,* mutters that gentleman, austere in the corner.
   I take him a drink to check his name.

Because daydreams should edify,
I'm not exactly happy with the company. He refuses
the cocktail. So we talk politics—prelatal abuse,
   the Star Chamber, theories of privy

   wolves roaming the episcopate.
Enough of London. What would he think obscene?
"I've read your *Areopagitica*; you're quite a libertine."
   We found it hard to be discreet,

   but all went well the next minute.
The afternoon vanished—his cambric tea fell cold
as I filled with ale. I unveiled the modern world,
   and he talked about his sonnets.

When night came our chat turned
serious. He spoke enthusiastically about Truth,
the richest merchandise, to defend his use of myth.
   The earlier crowds found their eras,

   and of course we were the last to go.
He'd object, but we were like two monks, through
with our harmonies and catenas, seeking some true
   knowledge of what we seemed to know.

# Rondeau for Plotinus

The things you said were said so perfectly
at times, sometimes I feel like Porphyry,
devoted one fed by your rarified thoughts.
All that's real is spiritual, so you sought
to split the barrier between degrees

of being. You wanted union with the One,
were said to *attain this end on four occasions.*
Fountain the soul can rise toward illustrates
the things you said

about the One's good spreading, and man akin to it,
emanation and return. This doctrine
glossed the Trinity, and to thank you I submit
these lines, which being ex nihilo shine
divinely beyond Nature, or so I interpret
the things you said.

# To the Author of *How to Be a Successful Artist*

Your title on the *Times* best-seller list
suggests you have a way of saying things:
avocation, or conviction to insist?
The need for peace surpassing understanding?
(Or just the lake house in Saratoga Springs?)
Ah, you must shine like a knife and be as keen
to puncture their hermetic questioning,
to best every great aesthete that's ever been!
So then, please explain: what exactly does it mean?

# From the Tarmac

The baby cries wildly
as the plane leaves the runway,
uproar struggling. Nose upward
at awkward angle, its power
drags to strangle each organ:
so naturally the child shrieks.
This might be his first break
from delicate rocking, her new
awareness of the world's pull,
compelling, bent to buffet.
As the wing drifts left, shingle
and aluminum appear,
thinning gray stents of highway,
the earthy green veinworks
spared by city planning.
Across the motley landscape
shadows of low-hanging
clouds spread out like long drapes,
or shapely silhouettes
in Victorian lockets. The
darkened spaces seem so still,
empty Main Streets, combines
silent, farmers and field help
napping through the afternoon,
peace beyond velocity,
and the child soon settles
into the old dream of home
again, fingers curled, having
survived the outer fervor.

# Intercession: For My Daughter

There pass so very many. Ones who come
through original darkness to join us here, helpful
and perfect, perfectly helpless like yourself.

These No People made holy just being,
in being known at all, as your recent heart
whose blue knee will genuflect for *x* many years.

If only to end the bending took one shape only.
No stillborn or tornado victim sleeping, to-do list
found the next week stuffed in a squirrel hole.

Nor steady drip that forms the most primitive
of timepieces. Fluid ceasing, then the alarm: no
more cotton-gowned invalid's middle way.

Unsuspecting little girl, may this world be always
too small for you, your last days long and still
not length enough. Differ from me, so often paralyzed

by how to fill another thousand hours. Never valiant,
but not the worst reply to living, either. Improve
my stewarding. Love the boredom and the grace you're given.

*Bless those born today,* pray the infant congregations.
*Bless those this day who will die,* chant the dying.
The only place, this passing. There are so many.

# Contrition: Midnight Message

As I turn out the last light, a beep
from the laptop; I feel a need to read it.
Your Thursday morning coffee friend
has sent a brief note—words curt, compunctious:
her grandmother's dying, means she'll miss
the time tomorrow. "Off to Buffalo. Sorry."
Facing you in bed, I nudge your shoulder.
*Mmmm, thank you . . . I always want to keep*
*appointments.* Your half-awake comprehension,
this graciousness at disappointment. Blessed
are the ones who can love the earth they inherit.
Please forgive the messenger, whose words hurt.
I turn toward the dresser in the darkness,
but you turn too, and put your face to my face,
and wrap your arm around me into sleep.

# The Advent Calendar

Through the ear the Word of God,
pressed on cardboard, impregnates
with dignity the sleeping Mary,
whose child, the creed says,
"was conceived by the Holy Spirit."

So the Church Fathers saw it,
and for portraits such as this you love
their resourceful escapes, the saving
image in the face of language.

It's true, mystery is captured
by the world we know, but does it
then diminish? No clever gesture meant
to cover, no Vatican fig leaf,
these constructions drive belief

to necessary crisis. They give dimension,
savagely, and manifest the questions
given up on. Take away the stars
and glitter from this Advent calendar

(found along a sidewalk sale in June,
dollar ninety-nine), what remains
are rows of squares. You're left
with only days, bare and perforated,
a liturgy of doors, perfect symbol.

Don't days, after all, amount to this,
lined up, surreptitious? You open
and examine them, you count them
and you count them down.

# Westward, in the Fading Moments of Any One Day

Late afternoon, and the sun setting lower,
floating on the horizon, the tree line
bearing its balmy weight. A strange light
surrounded us, the peninsula's hidden burn.
The back roads that led to Pescadero
rose and fell and carried us past orchards,
then twisted through dark redwood groves
so tightly we were almost carsick,
a threat that felt somehow romantic.
Maybe it anchored our evening to the real.
Maybe it made us vulnerable.
Since it all went well, it needs to happen
more often. And racing to the ocean,
the day all but gone, we noticed a hollow
where a stand of trees fell under the contour
of the last hillside. Twilight filled this place
with brimful sweetness, a landmark to map
what was out there, whatever would follow.

# The Snow Day

Night raged around us, cruel and furious
while we slept, and finally empty, it retreated
inward, as if cloistered, to surrender
everything it wasn't: the neighborhood
like one unified snowfield in the morning
calm and our son storming through the bedroom,
quick to bet me a donut, over my paper,
he could spend all day outside. This guy's
no dummy, doubling his chances through kids'
logic, heart set on the outdoors *and* the donut.

And from our perch at the corner of the bathroom
window you and I see this three-foot warrior
of last night's nor'easter once again draw
the toy guns of his hands, loaded with conviction,
to pelt the line of powder he's sent skyward.
Marshmallow in a snowsuit, insulated
madman, he is pure soul out there,
ignorant of all worlds except the one
primitive kingdom he's created. He removes
his ski mask and dumps snow on his own head.

Our other one enters, recently teenaged,
says we're stupid for standing on the toilet,
and peers skeptically toward the yard. "You'd think
this was the best day of his life," she says,
sneering. Her lanky gait reminds me of us,
our awkward latchkey days before the term
was demographic. It's the way her life becomes
less ecstatic—clothes are more important,
haircuts start to matter—the child leaves her
for good. Cold's cold: she no longer likes the weather.

So how could she find that joy, our older
girl, who's worrying about what clubs to join
at the school fair? Our younger's throwing
snowballs at the car. He moves like the first
black streak of tempera, careless on a prairie
of canvas, or a lone eighth note stalled
rebelliously above the scale, one beat remote
from the motif, and he plays, indifferent, rich,
distant from the riches, running in crazed
figure eights for hours and going nowhere.

## Longing, Lenten

The walk back, more loss. When I open the door
it's over, so I set to piddling: tidy
end tables, check the mail, draw a bath.
The restless energy finally settles
as I pass the mirror. I peer into it.
My nose touches glass. Not much left,
already effaced, not even a cross
to speak of. A smudge. A few black soot stains
like pinpoints on the forehead. The rest
of the blessed ash has vanished to a gray
amorphousness, to symbolize . . . not much.
Except a wish for those hallowed moments
to be followed by sustaining confidence.
Except spirit, which means to shun its listless
weight for yearning, awkward if not more earnest
prayer and fasting in the clear face of dust.

"The Garbage Eater": The speaker is a member of a group of mainly young people in the Berkeley area, so called because their ascetic lifestyle leads them to search for scraps in Dumpsters behind local businesses. They reject the worldly culture around them, including their families, in favor of a secret, scripture-based lifestyle. All the members, both male and female, wear their hair short, and the men often have beards. They wear very plain outfits, or even rags. Many believe this group to be a cult.

"The Little Flowers of Dan Quisenberry": Born in 1953, Quisenberry was a relief pitcher for the Kansas City Royals from 1979 to 1988. Known for his witticisms, he died of brain cancer in 1998. He also wrote poetry.

"An Appeal to the Ghost of Patrick Kavanagh": Among the greatest Irish poets of the twentieth century, Kavanagh (1904–1967) was born to a farmer and cobbler in Inniskeen, County Monaghan, and is best known for his long poem "The Great Hunger," which broods on the trials of Irish rural life.

"Trashy Elegy for the Queen of Shock Rock": Wendy O. Williams (1949–1998) was lead singer of The Plasmatics.

"Afternoon Pilgrims": Influenced as much by Virgil and Propertius as by the symbolists and surrealists, Miklós Radnóti (1909–1944) was one of Hungary's most important modernist poets writing between the world wars. He was called into labor three times during the Axis domination of Hungary. During a forced retreat in 1944, he was shot with twenty-one others and buried in a mass grave near Abda (in northwest Hungary). Two years later his body was exhumed; on it was found a Serbian exercise book in which Radnóti had copied his final—and some of his greatest— poems.

"Parousia": The title is a Greek word meaning "presence" or "arrival" and is used in eschatological contexts in numerous places in the New

Testament. A 1999 exhibition of Richard Diebenkorn's paintings at the San Francisco Museum of Modern Art inspired some of the content.

"Devotion: For Our Bodies": Acts of the Apostles 1:24 reads, "And they prayed, and said, Thou, Lord, which knowest the hearts of all men, shew whether of these two thou hast chosen . . ." (KJV).

"Papyric Fragments": The poem is loosely rendered from A. S. Hunt's and C. C. Edgar's *Select Papyri* collection (Loeb, 1932–34) and A. J. Malherbe's *The Cynic Epistles* (1977). The lacunae have been added by a capricious renderer.

"Bridal Cave": The epigraph is from Plato, *The Republic,* book 7.

"Tea with Mr. Milton": The author is quite proud of his plagiarisms from Milton's great essay *Areopagitica.*

green
press
INITIATIVE

Northwestern University Press is committed to preserving ancient forests and natural resources. We elected to print this title on 30% post consumer recycled paper, processed chlorine free. As a result, for this printing, we have saved:

2 Trees (40' tall and 6-8" diameter)
769 Gallons of Wastewater
1 Million BTUs of Total Energy
47 Pounds of Solid Waste
160 Pounds of Greenhouse Gases

Northwestern University Press made this paper choice because our printer, Thomson-Shore, Inc., is a member of Green Press Initiative, a nonprofit program dedicated to supporting authors, publishers, and suppliers in their efforts to reduce their use of fiber obtained from endangered forests.

For more information, visit www.greenpressinitiative.org

Environmental impact estimates were made using the Environmental Defense Paper Calculator. For more information visit: www.papercalculator.org.